In Bloom

Reyna Noriega

Also by the author:
Prose & Cons

In Bloom

In Bloom

A poetic documentary of the journey to higher self

Reyna Noriega

Reyna Noriega

Acknowledgments

This book is the sum of all the parts that contributed to my growth these past two years. I am thankful first and foremost to God, the Universe, my guides for giving me the foresight that this journey would be both necessary and fruitful. It has been a blessing to consult with you and be led by you.

To my family, my rocks. It is because of you I have the love and security instilled in me that allows me to go out into the world and follow my dreams, imagine greater. The love we share is something I could never take for granted. Mom, your strength, your confidence, you are the prototype and it brings me comfort knowing I have even a fraction of you in me. Papi, I hope you read this, I hope it inspires you. You following your creative dreams served as a blueprint for me, I hope I am returning the favor now.

Many friendships established and ended this year have also been a huge catalyst for this growth. Thank you all for inspiring me. For teaching me to love without possession, to let go. So many strong women surround me and inspire me. One way or another you are in these pages.

In Bloom

This is only the beginning, thank you to those that support my journey. I feel blessed at all times no matter what I am enduring because I am able to express myself through my art. This is how I am able to give back.

Let this serve as a blueprint, a reminder. You are not alone, the journey is long, the roads are rocky but you will perservere.

Be gentle with yourself. Listen to what your soul is whispering, the answers all lie within you, gravitate towards your truth until you are nothing but light and truth.

If you're reading this I love you, I hope you love you too.

Reyna Noriega

Table of

Part 1
A Flower Wilts
15

Part 2
A Seed Takes Root
89

In Bloom

CONTENTS

Part 3
The First Sprout
157

Part 4
The Flower Blooms
229

Reyna Noriega

In Bloom

For You,
for me.

Look how far we've come,
look how far we're going.

Reyna Noriega

Introduction

If you read my first poem collection, Prose & Cons, you know that it heavily revolved around my relationship with someone. It spoke directly to my blossoming love, uncertainty, loneliness, doubt, and a hoard of other feelings. During the dissolution of that relationship, I began to see more clearly that I was putting emphasis on all the wrong things. I began to see I didn't know everything I thought I knew. I was in a stage of becoming, of unraveling, unlearning, and rebirth.

This also speaks to someone, this also speaks to a time in my life. The greatest love and journey I've ever known...

It is me.

In fighting to find my way back to her and in many ways, meeting her altogether, so many weeds in my being needed to be plucked, so that I could bloom. As I began to dig into that soil, fertilize those roots, I saw that although on the surface things seemed to be just fine, the foundation, the internal mechanisms, were dry, depleted, and in need of nourishment.

This world makes it so easy to forget ourselves.

In Bloom

Our souls are screaming to be seen and felt and we stuff cotton balls into our ears to drown out the noise. We put poison into our bodies to combat the hunger.

This time was different. It started off mostly as a test, an experiment. I wanted to see what would happen if I turned the love I was always trying so earnestly to give away, inward. If I loved me just a little more... What could I do? Who could I be?

What I found is that like a flower, with proper watering, ample sunlight and just a little more care there were seeds inside begging to take root.
In a warm brown bed they struggled free and new life was born.

The last time I wrote to make sense of my feelings, this time I write to remember every last one, and maybe leave behind some type of blueprint or at least some comfort for all of us who will go through this journey and know, yes it is hard but oh, it will be worth it.

Like growing pains, remember when your shins and ankles were sore from growth? So will be your heart, your mind, your soul. The universe, your God, the energies that surround us, will stretch and contort you into something bigger and more beautiful than you've ever imagined, but only if you allow it.

Reyna Noriega

In order to allow it, you mustn't fear it.

Rest if you must.

Cry if you need.

But always-

Bloom.

In Bloom

A Story in 4 Parts

A flower wilts:
past, pain, recovery

A seed takes root:
preparation of the mind

The first sprout:
signs of growth

The flower blooms:
self love, awareness, and actualization

Reyna Noriega

part ONE

In Bloom

A Flower Wilts
One day, you're vibrant, you're on top of the world.

In that moment you imagine it will always be like this. Your chin is raised towards the sun. There is a song in your step, and it feels like the sun follows you, she shines only for you.

And then a cloud passes by, and she is blocking the view, and your color starts to fade, you then start to droop.

You use what is left to power your steps, but there isn't much left to sustain you.

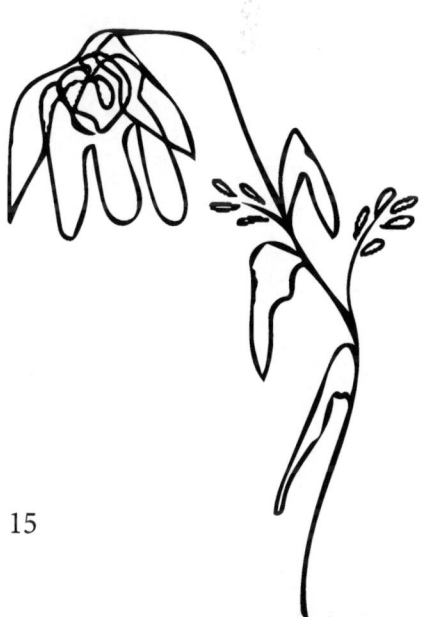

Reyna Noriega

In Bloom

you sucked me dry
my petals wilted
and forced me into the soil
but what you didn't know
what i didn't know,
was that the last of my seeds were still within
so i was buried
and i fought for the light,
and now i feel my stems stretching
i will soon bloom

—a flower wilts

Reyna Noriega

the love itself wasn't the con
not even the man in all his dishonesty
the con was the one i sold myself
that the fragments of his heart could be enough
that the passionless touch could be enough
that i could endure enjoying
the parts of myself i loved the most
alone
without my chosen companion
i believed i was meant to save
and i was,
but i was meant to save me

—post con

In Bloom

you've taught me a valuable lesson
the only person
i have any business
fighting for
is me

—lesson learned

Reyna Noriega

how convenient
you would twist our history
distort my motives
how is it you say
i tried to change you
that you weren't enough
when i was simply holding you
accountable
for the promises you made
for the person you said
YOU wanted to be
how am i the monster
for loving
so hard it hurt me
to see you give up
surrender to your shell
the ego
the darkness

—never again

In Bloom

it seems strange to say
we've "broken up"
can i really say we've broken up
if i never truly knew you
if we never really merged our lives?

—we were always broken

Reyna Noriega

ugly
our breakup was... ugly
it was crying constantly
cheeks sunken in
from the lack of appetite
squeezing the poor puppy
until she would squirm
to escape my sad embrace
it was being sick to my stomach
it was hoping, praying you'd come back
not yet knowing that was the last thing i needed
it was painfully and pitifully
crying to your dead mother,
asking her to look into my soul
at how much i loved her son
and to bring you back
not knowing,
you were out doing something so...
ugly

—this truth hurts

In Bloom

right now i don't feel like a winner
my eyes are pretty puffy
the bags full and kinda red
but i did,
i won
i was there
i was present
i felt
i loved
you hid
you lied
you left
but i was there
my heart
open and vulnerable for you
and maybe it was so big it scared you
so vast you feared getting lost
and you ran,
into her
but just like you told me
whoever folds first,
loses

—*i won*

Reyna Noriega

is there anything you can put on a heart wound to make it heal quicker?

—still rushing her

In Bloom

the first day i wake up without
checking my phone
it feels like an awakening
the first day i forget to miss you
forget to question all of my actions
all of my choices
the first day i feel hope
i just might get over this
i just might survive this

the revelation doesn't last long,
and now i'm tired again

— a different kind of tired

Reyna Noriega

now that i know the truth
our story is tainted
dirty
now i know the truth
all i want to say is
thank you
if i had given into the insecurity
the fear of the unknown
i wouldn't be who i am now
stronger and braver in the face of love

—make the most of it

In Bloom

we must cut ties
i wanted us to be better
than blocked numbers
and social media accounts
i wanted you to be better than manipulation
but you weren't

—blocked

Reyna Noriega

i know better now
but still i cry
because my belly is full
with love
and no good place to put it
so it bubbles up
until it materializes
into the tears
that kiss my cheeks,
kisses i long for from him

—i know i'll be okay, but it still hurts

In Bloom

are you even really there
if you aren't here
the way i need you to be

—*learn my love language or go*

Reyna Noriega

they can see the light in you
before you see the light in you
that's why they leave.

It's never been that you're not good enough

In Bloom

To my once best friend
Why is it so hard to admit when we are hurting.
In pain. Dissapointed.
For the longest time I stood unable to say, I am sad.
Who told you, you could just run off and create a new life,
Reinvent yourself, all without me?

The revelation made me angry
Resentful
Bitter.

But then I knew I had to choose gratitude.
Gratitude for all the things your presence taught me.
Gratitude for what your absence made me.
Hopeful that it did the same for you.

And I want to be happy for you, I am.
But there is a distance, a hole, I see in your eyes.
And I fear for you.
And because we were once best friends,
I know how it got there. I know all the vices you try to fill it with.
and I wonder if it will ever be filled.

—to you

Reyna Noriega

i ask for peace , for understanding
yet you keep trying to give me your tongue
i said i don't want us polluted by physicality
before we know intimacy
you agree, you understand
yet you deprive me of the things i need
as you focus on your own

—no more selfish lovers

In Bloom

what has happened to me
that i can't see love for me
when the air warms
with the promise of new love
i get excited
i yearn
and in the same breath i suppress,
i dispel the feeling
i can hold on to my fantasy of
spreading magic throughout the world
more than seeing
the most basic of human connection
in the cards for me
who has stolen my love for love
will i ever get it back

—damaged

Reyna Noriega

do they sell energy repellent?
i feel you buzzing around my ears
teasing at my neck
if i had energy repellent,
i'd make sure your memories
never resurfaced
whatever pesticide i can use
i need it
you are a detriment to my environment

—praying for amnesia

In Bloom

your mouth says not ready
but your heart says not me.

—and that's okay

Reyna Noriega

if it's not offered,
it's not promised
so don't you go saving space
for anyone not
holding a space
for you

—no more assumptions and projections

In Bloom

i'm trying
i can't
it's hard
trying so hard to let you in
i can't
it's hard
it's suffocating me,
and i can feel the hands around my neck
all i want to do
is to let go
i'm trying
it's hard
i can't
i know that i haven't let any one see me for a while,
not since him
and the aftershock,
the wall, is what caused me to lose him
teach me how to let go,
open up
i'm trying
it's hard
i can't

—but i really, really want to

Reyna Noriega

organic
i want everything to grow organic
no more rushing
not too much planning
i will plant seeds
i will nourish those seeds
then i will allow the earth to do its thing
i'll allow Mother Nature to do her thing
when i saw you i thought
you might be someone
i could grow with
so i planted seeds
i nourished them as you let me
and now i let the universe do her thing

—i won't force anything else

In Bloom

i just want to rest
it's new and i fear
maybe we should be dancing
laughing
telling tales of our youth
but for the moment, i need rest
my soul has been transient
shattered by non-mirrors
and now you seem okay
so for the moment
i need rest
i want to snuggle in real close to you
feel your chest move
rhythmically
because for this moment
we want the same thing

and i don't know how long we have

—let's rest

Reyna Noriega

why is it so easy to forget
the pain
when i see eyes
made to love
again

—snap out of it

In Bloom

i've never had
someone who feels so much like a friend
someone who could hear the moment
my body pleads for a soft kiss
or warm embrace
i've never had
someone hold me with such care
such tenderness
i've never had you

but there have been many you's
they all feel different
like magic
like fresh air
until the flog clears
and when it does
what will be revealed

—unsure

Reyna Noriega

why does loving feel like a disease
a curse
untreatable
just when i think i'm cured,
that the disease won't get the best of me
it's back in flowing through my veins
threatening,
lurking terribly close to my heart
and i realize just how defenseless i am

—feelings, make them stop

In Bloom

what is the plan
because right now it makes no sense
i'm summoning all my angels
looking at all the clocks
the sage burns in an old candle holder
i'm praying hard,
so hard
to make sense of it all
but right now i can't see the end
there is no clearing

—doubt is swallowing me

Reyna Noriega

you said you would do anything for me
and i need you to do that now
fix this
choose me
at least consider me
anything?

—my pleas fall on deaf ears

In Bloom

i did it.
i let you in
and you messed everything up anyways

—dating too soon

Reyna Noriega

soulmate you called me
and i believed you

— *ugh*

In Bloom

how could i be so starved for love
i confused your crazy
for intimacy
was it the Swiss spritzer
or the lemon scent in Positano
the light in your eyes
didn't radiate from your soul
they were the lights bouncing off the
Eiffel Tower
what was it that let me forget me?
your words, your touch, your patience

it's not men i don't trust,
its me

—praying for discernment

Reyna Noriega

stop saying fairytale
it comes out like a curse word against your tongue
and it hits me like a slap in the face
sharp and diminishing
i never asked for a fairytale
but an adventure
you and i stepping out into the world
growing and changing
helping and loving
hands joined but looking forward
to a future both separate and together
i asked you for a seed
to fertilize and build roots
a strong little thing that would grow bold,
with branches that house life and security
i didn't ask you to lose yourself and be melted into me
i asked that you see me
that you look deep and never stop looking
so that when you aren't facing me
you carry me in your spirit
what i asked for was real
instead you reduced it to a once upon a time fairytale thing

— i will never translate my love again

In Bloom

you couldn't look at me
and possibly think
i'd let you love me
one foot in,
one foot out
the door?

— don't insult my love

Reyna Noriega

i often question how i let this happen
how i let it get so far
but as the music plays
it takes me back
i heard these words for the first time when my mind was fresh
with possibilities of you and i
i learned the lyrics
with hope still to learn you
they touched me the way
i hoped you would
and it felt so good,
the way i knew you'd be
maybe if i had listened again
as things got out of hand
i'd realize the butterflies
had long been lost
but i hear it now,
months after
and it reminds me instead
in that moment i was alive,
i was hopeful
i wanted to feel what she spoke
but now i feel the song i once skipped
too sad, too fatal to relate

—musical memories

In Bloom

i give too much
and right now
i don't know if the answer is
to give less
or find someone
who gives just as much

—confused

Reyna Noriega

why do i want to tell you
our love story so bad
when you haven't even asked?

it is my story, not ours

—take ownership of your feelings and experiences

In Bloom

touch me with intention
or i may grow bored

your lazy fingers hold no magic
my hungry soul feels nothing

i'm counting the seconds
the tiles

release me already

—passion is a bare minimum

Reyna Noriega

i'm too good
for all of this
the hurt
the pain
the regrets
the blame
too good to be treated as a stepping stone
as replaceable

i'm too good to demand
to ask
to declare
too good to offer my story
or to hear theirs
too focused to ask the names of those closest to them

i'm waiting for the one
but if i'm too good
to be a friend
to the one i dream will love me
maybe i'm not so good
after all
maybe this is my toxic trait

—self awareness is key

In Bloom

the joys, the woes of being a woman
do they know what it feels like
struggling to accept your body
having it picked apart by outside eyes
and the minute you accept her
you love her softness
you love her curves
she changes yet again
something widens
something folds
and you begin the process all over again

—loving and re-loving is a cycle

Reyna Noriega

i've said it
and i'll say it again
don't touch me
if your hands are filthy
with indecision

—no more dirty hands

In Bloom

recurring themes
over and over
change
resistance
each lesson
increasingly intense
aren't you tired
of chewing me up
spitting me out
ripping me apart
flipping me inside out
i'm trying
why cant that be enough,
why cant here be enough?

—she wants more for me, even when i don't want more for myself

Reyna Noriega

you wonder why it's so hard
for me to trust
but you have proven
it matters not compatibility
or friendship
years
or moments
passion
or intimacy
the effortless switch
that allows you to compartmentalize
hide
ignore
the way you can treat us
as though we're all interchangeable
although you'll find out soon we are not
it scares me
it'll be a while before i can trust your kind

—reflections

In Bloom

you don't know me
in totality
you never will
completely

—i'm still learning me

Reyna Noriega

by the time these words are printed
it'll be too late for us
but too bad it never occurred to you
forever was never out of the question
you only needed to ask

—but if forever was meant for us, you'd already know this

In Bloom

"i am your friend and supporter despite anything else"

How could you know those words were said to me before. Same words. 3 times. 3 men. And all 3 times, less than a friend to me.

—you are not my friend, none of you were

Reyna Noriega

friends
just friends
you say it like it would be so simple
to make the transition
i almost believe you
it almost sounds nice
i wouldn't have to wonder
where you were
who you were with
because we'd be friends,
you would tell me
but would i want to know?
would that allow me to heal?
or would it be a band aid?

—friendship with you is a myth i won't sell myself

In Bloom

how do you heal the wounds
that are so deep
that have existed so long
that have roots so thick,
in trying to cut them you cut yourself

what can i do? what can we do?

—healing isn't simple or linear

Reyna Noriega

after all these years
i still pray
for one more chance
not to love you
although that would be nice
but this time i would speak
i would do so many things differently
if i knew you now
how i know me now
it is the only regret
that can make me feel so lonely
i consider going to you
and why don't i?

—i want a second chance

In Bloom

in moments like these
i remember them like ghosts
happy ghosts
drifting in my space
bringing their memories
only the ones i loved
or was robbed of a chance to love
the ones that still carry
a scent of what if
moments like this
that i want to bare my soul
that i want to say just one more thing
if it can bring you back to me

—maybe one day i'll be strong enough

Reyna Noriega

i'll be waiting for you
or the next stranger
that sets my soul on fire
the next one
that makes me take crazy risks
the next set of eyes
that i would cross oceans for.

—it always comes back to you

In Bloom

i'm so happy now
free
more in tune with me than i've ever been
but as i stare at this moon
laying as a perfect crescent
i wonder if you're seeing the same moon
4000 miles away
i long for you
i cry for you
and i wonder how there are still tears left

—is mercury in retrograde? i miss my ex.

Reyna Noriega

i say your name to remind myself
you were real
we were real

i've been feeling stuck here
frustrated
lonely
tired

they opened a Time Out Market here
like the one you took me to in Lisbon
the one you worked at
the one i fainted at
the one we shared kisses at

tears fell for the first time
in a long time

i had no idea how much i craved that release

and all of a sudden i'm mad at her
Why Universe?
why did you give me
everything i wanted
when i was too young
too dumb
to know what to do with it

In Bloom

i want clarity so badly
to make sense of this hole
that has lasted for four years
was it love?
or is this hole nothing more than a place
to hold my regrets

and i'm so fortunate to have loved you

an ocean away
my heart beats for you

but then i'm mad again.
you weren't supposed to give up
but i bought the plane ticket
i'm confused

you needed your city,
i needed mine
but i keep hoping there's a place in this world
that can be ours.

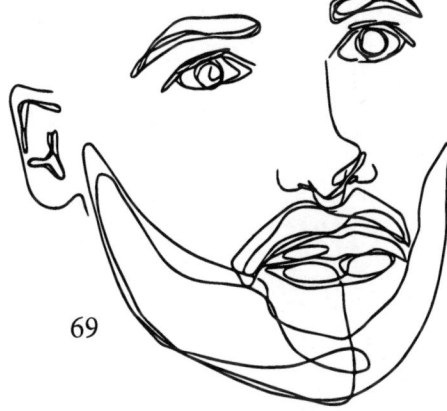

Reyna Noriega

i'm sorry i romanticized you
and robbed us of the chance
to know our truest selves

—regret

In Bloom

why does love leave me lazy
vulnerability leaves me spent
it feels like giving up parts of me
but do they even need to be kept?

—am i exhausted because i'm doing love wrong? can you do love wrong?

Reyna Noriega

the old me fighting
with the me to come
present me is tired
future me is greedy
she demands so much of me
so much i must unravel
unlearn
expose
i look for a distraction
or a loophole

—i am exhausted

In Bloom

have you ever wanted to be yourself so bad,
so so bad
and in that moment you realize
you don't even know who that is
anymore
having spent so much time
hiding
protecting
shielding
morphing
hardening
when it is time for once
to be nothing but who you are
you draw a blank

—i've wandered so far from me

Reyna Noriega

why do i always feel like this is a game
like if i master the tests
if i level up
then maybe i'll be rewarded with
something great,
someone great?

—it's not a test, stay present

In Bloom

i'm in a race against time
a race i created
a doom i've sentenced myself to
i understand the universe
her carefree whimsical prance
she rather glide through the flower fields
than run any marathons
yet here i am
pushing my body to the test
trying to prove that i am something
when i need not be anything but me
i tell myself go slow,
relax,
time isn't running out
yet every time the world cries
a new mission springs into my head
and i must act
i must break the shackles
that tie me into mediocrity
so that i can save them all
but in the meantime
i am killing myself

—drained.

Reyna Noriega

i let myself
fail
feel
and in these moments
i find my strength
my power

—feel every moment

In Bloom

you say you love yourself
but how do you prove it
if you continue to let
those that do not honor you
enter you
how do you show up for yourself
if not when it's time
to say no

—boundaries, practice them

Reyna Noriega

i know you want to grow
you want change
but understand who you are now
is enough
you are deserving of love where you stand

—keep working, but remember that

In Bloom

i want to be like a feather
light
careless
i want to be carried away by the wind
i want to be detached from any owner
while not forgetting my origin

—somedays i just ask for lightness

Reyna Noriega

my mind is so loud now
make it stop
so used to making plans
a pause feels unnatural
so sensitive to all that transpires
i have abused you
stretched you beyond repair
all i want is quiet now

—can i rest peacefully anymore?

In Bloom

i'm so sorry
but i'm afraid
i cant give myself to anyone
but me right now

if you can wait
although i won't ask
i think you'll like the me i find
much more

—excuse me while i evolve

Reyna Noriega

don't take this the wrong way
but—
i'm opening myself up to growth
not you
i have been picked up
tossed around
by different energies and entities
it hurts
i'm exhausted
i just really need to breath
regroup
recharge

— why i'm not ready

In Bloom

i was so afraid
they'd miss my magic
i didn't want them to see me
as beautiful
i tried to separate myself
from the constraints
of the aesthetic praise
so that i could focus on my roots
the flower that falls
unprotected without its stem
gets trampled

—but i'm both beautiful and strong

Reyna Noriega

my boundaries offended me
because i didn't love me enough

now my boundaries offend you
because you don't know love enough

—*boundaries*

In Bloom

so strange to think
and want the best for them
but all the while
they suppress hate and fear
of you reaching your potential
not realizing
the greatness they fear
are the barriers and doors
you wish to kick down
for them
why don't you want me to win?
why don't you want us to win?

—if one wins we all do

Reyna Noriega

advice is autobiographical
don't be out here
losing yourself
ready to self destruct
because you look for guidance everywhere
but within

—listen

In Bloom

i've been hiding her
for protection
for delayed gratification
but when she is tucked away
i'm not me
but merely a shell
a projection
but i'm going to let her out now
because she can not be ruined
or taken or diminished
she deserves to shine

— *she is strong, she is resilient, she is free*

part TWO

In Bloom

A Seed Takes Root

Sometimes even though a flower doesn't make it, before it wilts it drops some seeds.

And they rest there, in the soil, unsure of what to do.

And then the rain falls,

and they are touched.

They tremble

grow legs

and the seeds take root.

Reyna Noriega

In Bloom

planting seeds
watering seeds
speaking life into seeds
watering some more
i am the seed

—i am the seed

Reyna Noriega

why did it take you breaking me
for me to smile this wide
to laugh this loud
love this bold?
i guess i should say thank you

—thanks

In Bloom

i forgive you
for leaving
for lying
for stealing

—*from now on my battle is with me and no one else*

Reyna Noriega

this is the fun part
fun.
ironically the thought passes
through my head
as i feel the tears burn
and my tear ducts come alive

this is the fun part
the rebirth
the relearning
the reimagining

although the air reeks of death
and lovers lost,
it is also fragrant of next
of more
of greater

—i'll be okay again

In Bloom

i release all resentment
all records of wrongs
all need to prove
they're missing out
they lost
i won
it's robbed me of my ability
to be present
to love
to live
full and free
and right now
all i want
is to be free

—don't get mad, don't get even, disappear

Reyna Noriega

don't settle
i remind myself
i whisper the mantra
as my eyes catch his gaze
something passes through,
love maybe, but more than likely
it is lust
don't settle
you are a galaxy,
he is a mere gust of wind
it cannot possibly be enough
to throw you out of orbit

—you're stronger now

In Bloom

unloving you was easy, hard
easy because all it took
was seeing you
for who you really are
hard because
i had to ask myself
why it took so long to see

—this applies to so many

Reyna Noriega

it's a dirty job
this self love thing
i have to look at myself
open myself up
bleed to heal

but with every drop
i become more and more exhausted
how do i nourish myself
back—
not back
forward
keep pushing

—does the work ever end?

In Bloom

what comes next
what could go wrong
everything.
everything?
would i allow that?
no, never
then what do i fear?
meeting her.
she is a stranger
what does she look like ?
what does she like?
who are her friends?

—growth fears are real and they are overwhelming

Reyna Noriega

the illusion was
you don't need
you give
and give
and give
until there's nothing left
the reality was
you needed
you need
and only when those needs are met
can you give them your best

—love is rooted in self love

In Bloom

although you'd never ask
i forgive you
i hope i helped
though it wasn't my place
i wanted you to see this love story
i have been crafting
since i was a little girl

to all those that couldn't love me
i made space for you, i slowed down
i shouldn't have, i know that now
but how else
can i be sure not to miss true love
when she finally comes around?

we all have to believe in something,
i believed in you.

i saw you
the you before your ego took over
and for that i'm more grateful
than resentful

—making peace

Reyna Noriega

it's no one else's job to satisfy you
to fill that pit in your gut
the empty feeling of your soul
searching for meaning
that challenge is all yours
what are you going to do about it?

—stop postponing the work

In Bloom

derailed by attraction
i vowed never again
and when I said it, i believed it
because now—
now I know what i need
i need someone that chooses me
when they are lonely
and when they are surrounded by love
whether or not those around them are ready
i didn't want to be exalted or fetishized
i want to be accepted,
in my skin
it changes a lot

—reevaluating needs

Reyna Noriega

i'm actually not mad
at anyone who doesn't
do the work.
it is so soul crushingly hard.

i can understand
why one would choose
to stay the same
to make excuses

the work is plenty
there is no finishline
but it is so worth it

—tired still

In Bloom

kill her
or him
you
whichever parts
whisper still
you can't
you won't
you shouldn't
kill it
before it kills you

—homicide of the low vibrating mind

Reyna Noriega

you say you love yourself
how do you show it?
give yourself a bigger pot
water yourself daily
speak kindly
practice patience

—it's more than words

In Bloom

you only need to look up
forward
you only need to grow
stop trying to morph
to bend
to race
you only need the sun as a guide

—follow the light

Reyna Noriega

i don't tell my story
because why speak now
why the use the voice
i was unable to use to stop you
too afraid to make you feel like a predator,
when that was exactly what you were
isn't it enough
if i admit to myself
if i heal myself
i don't want to heal
being spectated by the world

— what's the point

In Bloom

i weep for the women everywhere
the ones that said no
the ones that couldn't
the ones that blame themselves
the ones that have healed but remember
the ones that self medicate to forget

forced to pick up the pieces they didn't break in
the first place

—triggered but moving forward

Reyna Noriega

your sacrifices were your own
your choices i held no part of
how am i supposed to show you
how much i appreciate them
if you hold it over my head
like a debt?

—give me kindness or nothing at all

In Bloom

what made you think that my body
belonged to you
that the fortress i created myself
was waiting to be dismantled by you?
was it because i called you friend?
because we laughed?
did you feel entitled to enter my space
violate my boundaries?
just when i was on a high
feeling so loved
surrounded by positivity
you shattered that
you made me all too aware
of what evil lurks
awaiting opportunity

— you are in fact a predator

Reyna Noriega

they owe us an apology
the artists
the dreamers
making our works worth
dependent on how much
of our trauma
we reveal
it has made me a masochist
oh the things i have put myself through
the things i have endured
i could have saved myself
but no
i needed to see it through
endure
i needed to fully indulge
i needed to feel
for the art

—because what is an artist without her story

In Bloom

the one
cannot meet me
if I refuse
to meet myself

— what are you afraid to find

Reyna Noriega

i want to write about philosophies
the human experience
i want to write things that will cure
heal our world
i want to do more,
be more
but it always comes back to love
can this be the key?

—confused

In Bloom

don't make me feel guilty for not falling for you
it's not me you want
you bait
and you'll take whoever bites back

—not interested

Reyna Noriega

i can move mountains
i can change the world
i can live by my own rules
but in love i fear
i worry
i cower
perhaps i just haven't practiced enough

*—love is in abundance, it flows through me
A mantra*

In Bloom

a partner
is smart
knows themself
in and out
doesn't stop uncovering
is an ally
my attraction is unquestionable,
they stop me in my tracks
yet i am calm,
patient
sure of myself in their presence
they are not entitled
they can keep up with my highest self
is an asset, not a liability
speaks life into me eternally
every merging feels like
wow —
you found me

— what do you really want? write it down

Reyna Noriega

in a dream
i see you so clear
your spirit
your aura

you touch
you taste
so sweet

there is peace
i've never felt
and passion
i've never known

electricity,
untamed electricity in your touch

power,
so much power
in the union

—i look forward to this

In Bloom

you seek
to take
to touch
to impress
but i don't want your greedy hands

—back to reality

Reyna Noriega

are you really alright or are you masking?
i only asked because i need to be asked
except no one is the wiser
so often we navigate the world
one smell,
one song,
one vision away
from running smack into our trauma.

—i wish there was a better way to ask

In Bloom

you're hiding, don't hide
your beautiful parts i feel them retract
i want to feel them
see them
experience them
but you won't let me
you aren't ready to share them with me
then why do you come?
why do you touch?
take?
taste?
if you aren't willing to feed me,
fill me
i don't need the things you think I need
i just need you,
but you,
you have yet to find.

—i hope you find yourself

Reyna Noriega

my ego decided to wake me this morning
she's concerned with everyone else
how we measure up
are we doing enough?

forgetting all that i've evolved from
causing me to overthink
to seek validation

—my ego is a liar

In Bloom

surrender
i've been learning
surrender
when my thoughts get loud
when i'm filled with worry
uncertainty
i surrender

—even that is difficult

Reyna Noriega

i'm not giving any more advice
i'm only meant to help you find you

—i can't save you from yourself

In Bloom

life is hard
choose the path of least resistance
go where there is
Love

—life's to hard to force anything

Reyna Noriega

life's too hard to force anything,

In Bloom

go where there is LOVE

Reyna Noriega

the concept of selfishness
for me,
it showed up a little different
it didn't mean breaking hearts
and running over people
it meant saying no more
to what didn't serve me
going out less
moving with intention
or not at all

—these are the selfish years

In Bloom

what's in a name
for me it's queen
but time and time again
i was content with being a servant
time and time again

why did i not require
they respect the throne?

because i hadn't built it yet
i hadn't decided
what my kingdom would look like
what the fortress would keep out

—time to build

Reyna Noriega

and when you think of me
i hope it
h—
heals
i hope it heals
that is growth
i no longer want my absence
to torture you

— wishing bad on you would stunt my growth

In Bloom

be careful
people will pull from you
any parts of themselves
they haven't healed

because you love them,
you'll let them
not even feeling it
as it erodes parts of you

—preserving what's left

Reyna Noriega

would you speak
to your friends
your mom
your boss
the way you speak to yourself?

please stop.

—handle with care

In Bloom

one thing i've realized,
people love it when
they know what to expect from you
but i'm not really a fan
of being easily consumable
they will chew you up
spit you out
and you won't even be able to recognize yourself

—don't change for them

Reyna Noriega

it's not enough just to manifest
make a wish
write it down
get your heart right
get your mind right
get your body right
watch the fog clear

—it must all match

In Bloom

when you love people
not possess them
when you lose all sense of entitlement
you allow them to grow
to change
maybe they don't stay
maybe they never return
but you'll be okay

—love without limits

Reyna Noriega

i'm scared because this is big
much bigger than me
so it's times to lean into that fear
and choose honor and gratitude instead
that i was chosen
we were chosen,
let's do what we came here to do

—fear isn't a finish line

In Bloom

i have learned how to look within
now I must go back out
and experience the world

—balance

Reyna Noriega

take the leap,
and when you do remember to look around
not down at how fast you're falling
or how close you're coming
to crashing
look around,
stay parallel

don't miss the blessings on the way

—be present

In Bloom

i wanna save the world
says my young
arrogant
ego driven self
i picture myself
silk flowing
hair blowing
smiling from ear to ear
i would snap my fingers
open a few centers
sprinkle some money
and alas —
i would be savior
until i started to do the work
and saw not only
was it not just me
but it wasn't me,
not about me at all

—ego has no place in philanthropy

Reyna Noriega

seek to explore
not conquer
not possess
i feel the difference in your fingertips
one is coarse and swift
i prefer inquisitive and electric

—love me thoroughly or not at all

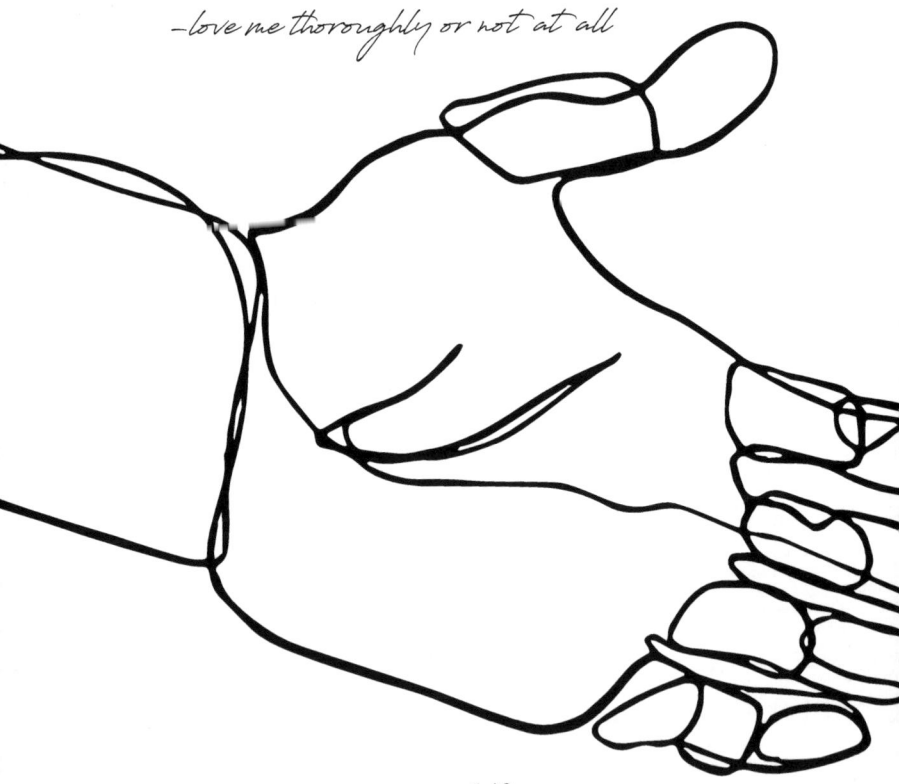

In Bloom

you will find yourself
and lose yourself
many times over
in this lifetime
never stop searching

—it is constant

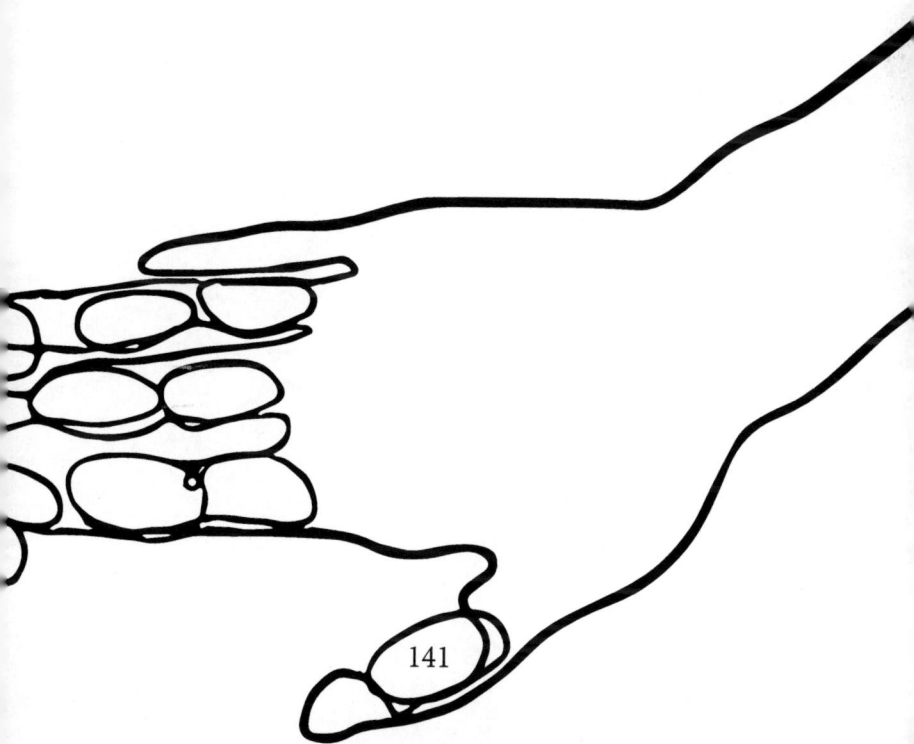

Reyna Noriega

does one ever grow tired
of the what ifs
the hypotheticals
the dreamt up conversations
the imagined caresses

—too much daydreaming

In Bloom

your triggers are telling
listen to them.

—you're being called to grow

Reyna Noriega

clean your house
when you don't
energy settles like dust
collects in the corners
hosts spiders and creepy crawlers
open the windows
let in light
fire up some candles
dance with your broom
welcome better

—cleaning as self care

In Bloom

be intentional about caring for your body
your health
the things you already possess
the spaces you occupy
before asking for more

—it's already enough or it will never be

Reyna Noriega

stay faithful in the storm
it is not a test
it is not a punishment

—preparation

In Bloom

neglecting what you have
for what you'll have next
will only leave you with nothing

—*learning appreciation*

Reyna Noriega

i need you to touch me
like every layer i let you pull back
is an exclusive, private gift
like only you
its ever been
or ever will be
fighting for a taste

—silent needs

In Bloom

how dare i
waste moments on fantasies
and naughty dreams
when i have so much
work to do

—avoidance

Reyna Noriega

i spend alot of time by myself now
thinking
listening
reflecting

i reflect on my growth
fantasize about love
imagine my future
my beautiful future

how will i get there?
i start to plan on the post-its
more fantasizing

"wanna go out tonight?"
-no i'm busy
busy, busy, busy

busy doing nothing
busy doing everything
busy getting to know me.

—isolation mode

In Bloom

i don't know what to do
my face is lubricated by lost dreams
my soul aches
my hands are in a frenzy
in a moment of despair,
desperation & vulnerability
i call my mom
i forget how embarrassed i am to admit
that i still feel
i still long
she gives me a simple solution
and for once i don't question her

—tell him

Reyna Noriega

i wish for you

In Bloom

11:11

everytime

Reyna Noriega

I'm not sure why these thoughts are suddenly haunting me.

I tell myself it's avoidance.

Resistance.

A way to distract myself from the greatness I'm meant to achieve.

But you rest there in the back of my head. I don't know what to do with this... regret?

I've never felt that before, don't want to feel it now, I don't have TIME to feel that now. I wish your ghosts would just let me be.

But as much as I want to say that it's irrational and it will pass, I remember some forgotten quality about you.

Your patience.
Your smile.
Those hands.

In Bloom

Oh, those hands. They held, they caressed, protected.

Worst of all, each level I ascend to, I can see you even more clearly. The ultimate partnership I lost.

I pray aloud--
"God please send someone, anyone, to prove that this feeling was just a feeling and it can be duplicated"

But they never come, or they never do.

They don't have your self awareness, your strength or maturity.

The only man I've ever met that speaks more languages than me.

I have to let this go.

But what if I can get it back?

Reyna Noriega

part
THREE

In Bloom

The First Sprout
A yawn in the morning, a crack of the back, you stretch so that your wings may choose to unfold. They didn't yesterday, but will they today?

If not they will eventually, and thats okay.

At least you have your peace.

Reyna Noriega

In Bloom

me and my plants,
we can all grow here

—new beginnings

Reyna Noriega

noise
static
a robber
a thief
voices
whispers
sometimes screams
get out of my head
i only want peace

—there are still dark days

In Bloom

you're playing a dangerous game
you don't know yourself
but you're trying
to heal the world
trying to save others
you are just as lost as the rest
the world is not your project

—note to self, fix you FIRST

Reyna Noriega

i just want to be around people
that speak my language
so tired of translating
so tired of telling my self to be quieter
no more having to slow down
dumb down
all that is me

—*finding my tribe*

In Bloom

they did the best they could
with what they had
but new knowledge is within reach
and if you can leave behind
what was
we can all climb

—rethinking

Reyna Noriega

beware of the trap
the comfort
that tells you
you're done
you know enough
you've learned enough
you're the you-est you you'll ever be

—keep growing

In Bloom

it's not enough
to think it
to wish it
to dream it

when you feel
it, when you act
on it   that's when
all begins to
change

—take a step

Reyna Noriega

it's no one else's job
or rather,
right—
to decide who you are
how much space
you're allowed to occupy

—decide and expand

In Bloom

i call this chapter:
i finally know my purpose and worth
now when and how
do i shout it from the mountaintops?

—when does imposter syndrome go away?

Reyna Noriega

cancelling all my plans
my ideas need me
right now

—*choosing me*

In Bloom

Do the work.
Do the work.
Do the work.
Do the work.
Do the work.
Do the work.
Do the work.
Do the work.
Do the work.
Do the work.
Do the work.
Do the work.
Do the work.
Do the work.
Do the work.
Do the work.
Do the work.
Do the work.
Do the work.
Do the work.
Do the work.
Do the work.
Do the work.

—that is all

Reyna Noriega

we are breathing and believing
and i feel her so near now
we are not there
but we're closer
and getting
closer
each and every day

—so close

In Bloom

oh love
growth is not all pretty
there will be times
you'll need to
get on your knees
and pull weeds

—have gloves ready

Reyna Noriega

this time when i cried
it was with gratitude
an emptying of all the feelings
that had accumulated
during a 3 week romance
there's nothing
i've feared more than disappointment
but i allowed myself to feel
and to enjoy
knowing that at the end of your stay you might not
choose me
and when you didn't
i said goodbye
and thank you
knowing i lost no pieces of me,
crying
because this is a turning point
i will look back on these tears with gratitude
knowing all the curses they broke

— a turning point

In Bloom

i've learned boundaries are important
because if you don't
the ends are ugly—

loving hard is not love at all
if it features complete disregard of self
it is not kind and benevolent
if you forget to protect the source
if at the first sight of betrayal
you feel spent and tired
because you forgot to save some things for you
and now they have thrown it all at your feet
and spat at it so carelessly
at that moment you will see
where you went wrong
loving too hard
caring too much
love alot,
care a lot
but only with what is left after loving you

—when "friends" show their true colors

muse
why didn't i realize sooner
everything i make
i get to keep
we can last for ever
even if you aren't with me

—love is energy, energy never dies

In Bloom

the way she cared for me
taught me how to care for her

i tended to her seeds and they served me

—*on finding sisterhood*

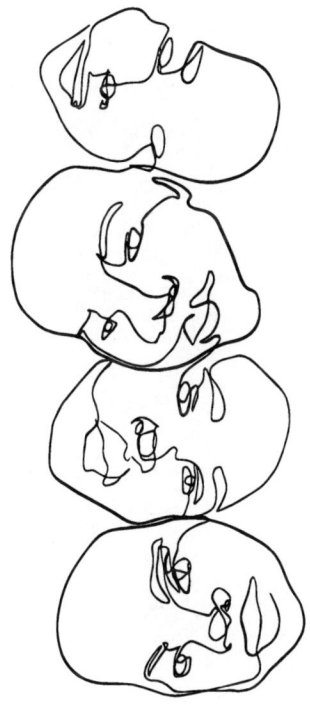

Reyna Noriega

every time they push me over the edge
i'm sent plunging deeper and deeper
into me

and it scares me
here they are
barely scratching the surface
and here i am conquering more of me

how can i expect to find my equal
is there anyone out there being prepared
just as much as me ?

—they just can't keep up

In Bloom

because what the world likes will change
make sure you like you
because their definition of greatness will change
be sure you define you
because everything they give can be taken away,
make sure you sustain you

—self reliance

Reyna Noriega

hello old friend
i was prepared to shed skin
to grow
to reach whatever potential
whatever plans
my God had laid out for me
but outgrowing you hurt

i have had to suppress
my feelings of being used
and justified them with
what i gained
when i lost you
what the clear site afforded me

—losing people is still uncomfortable

In Bloom

love your self
you keep trying to pour
the little bits you've salvaged
into others more lost than you
because you are love
and love lives within you,
you will survive it
but love yourself

—this applies to friendships too

Reyna Noriega

the thing with gut feelings,
they will continue to confuse you
until you learn the language
it's an intimate one
for only you
until then
we think they are clues
of something definite
but instead they warn you
go slower
speak internally
consult your angels
surrender
readjust course
reevaluate

—listen

In Bloom

i get it now
i kept trying to talk to you
and him
and her
and them
but i needed to speak to me
i needed to work on me
i needed to love me
and accept me

—lessons learned

Reyna Noriega

stop fighting the current
save your strength
for the work you must do
there is a path so beautifully paved
just for you
and all you must do to find it
is surrender

—here's that word again

In Bloom

how do i translate my love
in a language you can understand
i'm sorry your generation failed you
i'm sorry they didn't teach you
to love yourself
fill yourself
be selfish
you look to us for answers
for the love you so selflessly poured out
but what i have to give
can never replace
what you need to give yourself

i am still blooming
i am still learning
and if i break off my petals
and boil you a tea
you'd still spit it out
say it was too hot
and so the ache remains

—for our mothers

Reyna Noriega

i found a new life
and forgot about my power
the intrinsic instinctive power
the power of woman
the strength'
the erotica
the creation

i hid behind my newfound strengths
and forgot effortlessly
my power runs through me

—you are divine for all the reasons

In Bloom

i pray you find
happiness that is sustainable
happiness only dependent
upon you

i hope you go where the sun kisses you,
where the air makes you feel alive
where your moments don't have to wait
for others to choose you

i hope you choose you
i hope you choose happiness
every moment
of everyday

—it is yours to claim

Reyna Noriega

do plants feel like this
when all that energy
compacted into a little seed
must be set free

when the roots begin to span out
contort
stretch
when the sun beats down
when the droplets kiss it
when it starts to bend over
and the air whispers
"i wont give up on you"
and gives it the strength
to bear one more season

but i'm so damn tired
of bearing seasons
making it through
i want my flowers
i'm ready to bloom

—i'm ready

In Bloom

after so many lessons
after learning to navigate
with the highest sense of consciousness
when calling on my guides
my angels
in a time of surrender
they'd tell me to revert
go back
reclaim my innocence
reclaim my optimism
reclaim my joy
stop navigating
just exist

—*back to basics*

Reyna Noriega

thank you to the ones
that have left the breadcrumbs
i have followed
and learned
and they've led me
here

—this too is a blueprint

In Bloom

the heavens opened
with an answer to my prayers
a rumble i interpret as processing
and then the water falls
lubricating my dreams
nourishing them for growth
then the clouds part
and the sun is revealed
and i know that all will be well

—rain is cleansing. rain is transformative

Reyna Noriega

i have wanted to cry every day now
i am on fire
there is a current passing
through my body
exploding out from my eyes,
my mouth,
my fingers
especially my fingers

it feels like in this very moment
anything i touch
will turn to gold
so i capitalize on this moment
shield my self from the noise

—stay focused now, it counts

In Bloom

the unfolding so organic
at times i take for granted
how much has happened
and changed
since the last time we met

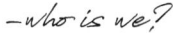
— who is we?

Reyna Noriega

be bigger
be bolder
for too long
you have held the fire
within
to not offend
to not burn
let the fire rage
it will warm their souls

—we don't play with fire, we become it

In Bloom

empower yourself
don't give anyone that power over you
you don't need permission
give someone else the job
to lift you up
and they'll drop you everytime

—a harsh reminder

Reyna Noriega

speak your truth LOUDER
don't whisper
let their ears bleed

—*louder*

In Bloom

succulent
so full
you need for nothing
you wait
to be watered

—i want to be like a succulent

Reyna Noriega

what are you willing to give up to be great
earnestly you say everything
your soul even
but don't be foolish
you only need to give up
the parts of you
that weigh you down
honor your body
honor your mind
let greatness become you

—it's always been inside of you

In Bloom

a quick pause--

to reflect.

So much has happened, so much has changed. You're pursuing your dream, from the outside looking in it appears you're living that dream, but there is still so much fear, tears, and uncertainty.

Although stronger, your heart is still broken and confused. The loneliness leaves room to reflect, to imagine bigger and better love.

But why do they still call? Why must they still haunt you?

Your ideas of success and wealth are changing. Currency is nothing to peace, but you are coming to understand your worth and value, and getting your fair pay.

So much is unraveling, revealing itself. You're exhausted. Carry on.

Reyna Noriega

you're nice
you're trying
but i don't like your energy
trusting my gut on this one

—self preservation

In Bloom

having it all
means saying no ,
what a strange concept

—another lesson in self preservation

Reyna Noriega

you want to change the world,
let's start here
the love you've been pouring outward
pour it in you instead
until your cup runneth over
and your whole body feels new
then i want you to look to your left,
your right
what small things can you do?
is there a friend you can speak life into ?
a helping hand you can give?
you want to be the greatest
but the greatness is already within you

—big dreams take small steps

In Bloom

ideas
dreams
they don't happen by accident
they are brought to you
sent to you
the universe has chosen you
she knows you are worthy
do you believe her?

—it's time you believed

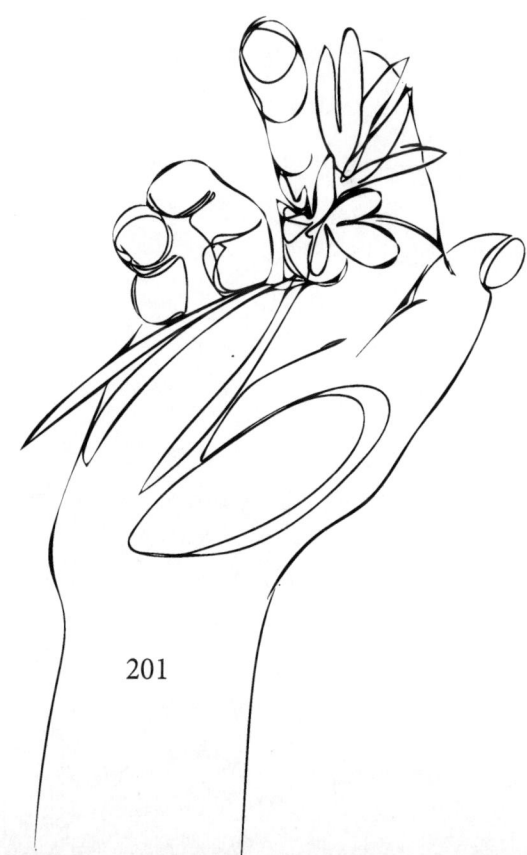

Reyna Noriega

say no to say yes
yes to more
yes to better
yes to you

—no

In Bloom

i will not be easy to consume
put down your mallet
put away your blender
come with an appetite
or don't come at all

—come hungry

Reyna Noriega

release
unto the universe
i release,
release,
release

release

In Bloom

i've done some pretty crazy things for love
i've been brave in the right and wrong ways.
and now i'm testing my bravery in a different way
i'm betting on me
so this chance i'm taking on you
it's actually me
trusting i'm brave enough
strong enough
to love
with no guarantees

—love yourself, trust yourself, so you can love others without possession

Reyna Noriega

afraid to reach my highest self because even now
they say they are intimidated by me
until i realized it was a shield
my greatness could ward off
those not worthy of me.

—rise

In Bloom

you glow
skin so gold
hidden corners
and soft curves
winding hills
valley deep soul

—self appreciation

Reyna Noriega

i am ready
i know i've said it
i've thought it
i've tested in my past
but this time i'm ready
to receive all you have for me
to be bold in the face of compromise and say NO!
i am ready to dance with the song of new love
you have waiting for me
i will not bend
i will not break
never again
this time, i'm ready for the real thing.

—but when is one ever really ready

In Bloom

blindfold me from perceptions of you
i want something new
that is neither reminiscent of the past
or an expected future
but better.

better in its uniqueness
better for its mystery
better because i'm better,
i know better.

—no expectations

Reyna Noriega

making space
i've cultivated such a safe space
and now
i must make space

for you?

—whew

In Bloom

hate is nothing more than us being lazy
too lazy to learn
to expand our understanding
so we look for clues
a deviation from what we believe to be "normal"

i want them to stop being lazy
stop relying on the headlines
stop hiding behind apathy
i need to make them see

—this matters more than my love life

Reyna Noriega

there are things to do,
a world to save
so my feelings will have to wait
if in some way
at some point
both are possible,
i'm open

—conflict of interest

In Bloom

I'm happy
I read two books this month
I got new plants
I painted
I danced
I'm happy

—small wins

Reyna Noriega

the work starts within
uncover whats been covered
what lies hidden in corners of your mind
heal
be honest
be loud

—something aches, time to figure out what it is

In Bloom

through all my healing work
and introspection
my past continues gnawing at me

could it be time
all these year later
to finally speak up for myself

to speak my truth?
am i ready for the repercussions?

i guess i'll find out...

-here goes nothing

Reyna Noriega

They've opened a Time Out Market here in Miami. I'm going to the opening tonight and all I can think about is you.

I want to be very clear, I love you. That has always been very real to me. It was clear after 4 days and still is after 4 years.

I want to try again. To know you as the man you've become and for you to know me, as the woman I've found and become since leaving you. Mature and independent.

If the opportunity arises, I want to try. Wherever in the world and whenever the universe allows us to be together again, that is my wish.

- whatsapp 05/08/2019 12:22 p.m **EST**, 5:22 p.m **GMT**

In Bloom

i knew i had grown
i knew i could differentiate love
when i realized
i would do anything to be with you
to feel your love
except lose myself
except pause my dreams
my work

we could find a way
any way,
but not at the expense of shrinking me

—conditional

Reyna Noriega

before i open this message
before i read your response
i take a moment
i inhale
i exhale
i say a prayer
i sing a song
and i ask for grounding
surrender
peace
that whether you respond in favor
or your reality is different than mine
i make sure i'm ready to handle both
with grace
with openness
that i won't let you take me too high
or drop me too low
my need for peace is bigger than my love for you

—i say this with pride, the healthy kind

In Bloom

the surrender i was looking for
came from action
the clarity i needed
was born from a mess
of tears and confessions
of less than ideal responses
fluttering angry butterflies
but in the morning i was free

—and the freedom was worth it

Reyna Noriega

life is like that game
at the county fair
as long as you keep shooting water
into the hole
you progress
it doesn't matter how fast you were once going
because if you stop
lubricating that spot
you will cease to advance
and you will be passed

—eye on the target

In Bloom

i wish someone would've told me
joy comes from within
i wish they would've told me
you have to know who lives there first
i wish they would've told me
joy and acceptance brings clarity
i wish they would've told me
the joy isn't in being somebody,
but in knowing ones self
i wish they would've told me self esteem
and confidence,
isn't something you're born with or without
but a relationship you will cultivate
your whole life

—so i'm telling you

Reyna Noriega

and then i decided
it was time i treat
my mind right
my body right
my hair right.
all the things
i looked in the mirror
wishing to see
differently
instead,
care for those things
REALLY care
and see the difference

—change is coming

In Bloom

hello beautiful
you are strong
you are smart
you are ready
resilient

i am so glad to see you
i can't wait to be you

—conversations with my higher self

Reyna Noriega

the only way to improve your craft
is to improve yourself
create a relationship so intimate
the depths you explore are reflected in the art
the light you have found is projected out.

—let it pour from the inside out

In Bloom

You have a big heart and an affinity for fairytales.
You deserve love, and it's coming, but remember to slow down.
Don't romanticize reality because your overactive imagination has already spun your happy ending.
Ask the questions that matter--
Do you share the same considerations?
The same expectations for the future?
Will you raise your children with the same values?
Will you raise children at all?
Does this person know how to love?
Has he been shown love?
Has he spent time loving himself?
These things matter,
And don't you ever, not even for a second,
Think a spark can make up for asking these things.
Hear no even when laced in empty promises.
See hope at the other side of hard conversations.
Find joy, hold on to it,
And hold on to you.

—note to self

Reyna Noriega

REMINDERS

8:00 AM

I surrender and I accept my healing

9:00 AM

I am ready to receive all the universe has planned for me

10:00 AM

I understand and embrace my power

11:00 AM

What I desire is already mine

In Bloom

REMINDERS

12:00 PM

Listen to lead, step into your leadership

1:00 PM

You are you, that is a gift. Don't compare

2:00 PM

You welcome capacity and abundance

3:00 PM

Focus on joy

part FOUR

In Bloom

The Flower Blooms
One day, the mirror brings peace. It no longer reminds you of demands that must be made. Of what you lack, or what's missing.

One day the person in the mirror staring back at you, is enough. The reflection may not have the grocery list of things you requested, but something about the glow in your eyes isn't sadness or longing. It is a twinkle.

It is promise.

Reyna Noriega

In Bloom

please live loudly
stop trying to occupy
the least amount of space
you're not doing them any favors
by denying them your light

—light them up

Reyna Noriega

i am not them
they are not me
their paths do not determine mine

—stop comparing

In Bloom

if there is one thing
one word that you keep
find your voice
so that no sound in the universe
can overpower that
of the one that speaks
and guides within
no tornadoes of false prophecies
can sweep you up
throw you off your path
learn you,
rely on you

—find you first

Reyna Noriega

i can't believe i get to live this life
i think, as my tire lights blare
because i've neglected my car
because time
because money
my bank account running low

but i get to live a life
marked by a vision for me
for more than just me
as i am now
grateful i can feel this all over me
and inside me
bubbling so close to the surface now

and so now
here
even before the abundance manifest
I Am Grateful.

—gratitude brings me peace

In Bloom

the day
you plant the seed
is not
the day
you eat the fruit

but,
the day you plant the seed
tend to it--
is the day you've decided
to start

—start now

Reyna Noriega

maybe i'm addicted to new
new smells everywhere
the man, his scent
the new restaurants he takes me to
new taste, not only food
but those on his lips when
they meet mine for the first time

i have now found
i am not weak to the man
i am addicted to adventure
but adventure i can create for myself

she and i go see new movies
and we laugh until our belly hurts
we try new foods with our girlfriends
feeling safe rather than giddy with butterflies
the feelings last longer
they are not tainted
but there is still so much new

— i am really enjoying life right now

In Bloom

it worked
the meditation
you sent me 2 minutes 27 seconds
of your voice
you explained you didn't feel the same
i don't blame you,
i don't feel rejection
i feel free
we are both open to friendship
and that too can be beautiful
romance isn't the only blessing

—2 minutes 27 seconds and i am free from what ifs

Reyna Noriega

now this is what true freedom feels like
true surrender
today is a new day
a day of firsts
the first day i feel i can see clearly
like my heart and i speak the same language
she has been trying to reveal to me
the truths i had been avoiding
your rejection brings me so much joy
i love you more for it
but not in that way—
our story is now written and archived
a new page turns

—why didn't i try this sooner

In Bloom

what is this
why does it all make sense
yet no sense at all
my eyes forever opened
my consciousness on a high
traveling on a thin line suspended in the air
but i'm not scared
i don't feel wobbly like i did
with both feet on the ground
i feel my wings
i'm standing in my power

—this is the shift

Reyna Noriega

I don't know what triggers it, or if you can plan or prepare for it. In actuality, every step I took prepared me for it. I explored my interests. I watered my desires, even when it felt like it would be unfruitful. I knew just enough about my self to know my strengths and weaknesses, and still when it came it disrupted everything I thought I knew.

In an instant it changed me in a way I still don't understand. At a gas station preparing to refuel all of these synapses started to happen.
I understood the common goal within all my ideas. I understood my intrinsic needs and unique power. An additional eye opened and I understood. I saw. The why. The how. The when.

I would save.
I would create.
I would do it now.

My voice was unique. Every single fiber of my being came together to create a human tool for change.

In Bloom

It gave purpose to everything, my joy, my pain my experience. Literally everything.

There was a reason I had to continuously evolve. There was a reason I had to fight, to speak. My existence would heal, my existence would save, my existence would change.

Reyna Noriega

i never win anything
i used to think it was because
i was unlucky
unfavored
but she loves me so much
she gave me the strength
the foresight
to go and get
and not wait for it to be given

—i am the winner of my own race

In Bloom

with the petals that fall
i make pot-pourri
they are fragrant with lessons learned
they are intoxicatingly telling
of growth
of despair
of greater truths

—*it's all me*

Reyna Noriega

you have something they don't
remind yourself of this
everytime you scale your limitations
by the limitations of others

—uniqueness is a gift we all possess

In Bloom

sometimes you have to think of your higher self
as a completely other being
talk to her
call upon her
consult her
until you become her

—i call her Queen

Reyna Noriega

offering myself the gift of
patience
mercy
and rest
as i prepare for the glow up

—rest is a privilege i may not always have

In Bloom

we don't operate from lack anymore,
love is all around us.

—*abundance*

Reyna Noriega

what did i do to deserve your favor
why do you whisper to me
the lessons so perfect
made for only my comprehension
even when it hurts
even when it threatens to contort me
beyond my comfort
i trust
and i feel your favor

—i feel chosen

In Bloom

for the first time
in a long time
maybe ever--
i am content
i want no other life
no future brighter
than my present

—gratitude + presence

Reyna Noriega

more days like today
more realizations that life
is so damn beautiful
more days of stopping
smelling
gazing
appreciating
more gratitude
more love
more everything

—i am happy for no reason, which is the best reason

In Bloom

open
leave the green light on
stay open
to all the universe wants to send you

—stay open

Reyna Noriega

she listens to me
all i need to do
is whisper
dream
and she listens
she knows the desires of my heart
even the ones i dare not admit to myself
she listens

—the universe is all knowing

In Bloom

letting the universe be my teacher
living in release
constant surrender
too many times
i chose to stay rooted
in my perceptions of false truths
only to need hurricanes to set me straight
instead,
now i wade in a sea of patience
calm
truth
so she only needs to ripple
to love me
to move me

— no more learning the hard way

Reyna Noriega

where i see hope
others see cages
and now i know
that's why you chose me

—theres work to do but it isn't impossible

In Bloom

i said yes
to me
my higher self

i had been bargaining for so long.
can i?
should i?
do i want to?
were the little visions and inklings i got for more
a reflection of a destiny
or a selfish need?

it came time to push beyond the noise
beyond the doubt
and elevate

—it's time

Reyna Noriega

i hid behind a false cloak of uncertainty
so that those plagued would be placated
by my kindredness
but really i was sure of who i was
and what i was meant to be for so long
and it was only when i stepped up
and stepped out
i could help those i was shielding
those that would rise in my presence and not
crumble and cower in the shadow

— *i am fully me, and i hope it inspires you*

In Bloom

and then one day
you wake up
you're free
you've changed
there is a song in the air,
a song of promise
you can dream again
you can want
you imagine
and you know that
because you can see it clearer now
in your mind
it will soon be yours.

—*bloom so beautifully
your reflection shocks you*

Reyna Noriega

they don't tell you about the curse
that comes with the gift of sight
once you see all the universe has to offer
you also inherit the burden of the lost souls

those weighed down by fear
anchored in place by the excuses
convinced they cannot
when you know
they can,
we all can

—it hurts to see you settle

In Bloom

this ones for us
that felt we had to be
watered down
diluted
to be ready for love
i hope you now know
you deserve to be loved on loud

—own it

Reyna Noriega

i had to apologize for frustration
getting the best of me
for the times patience wasn't apart of me
and i got so caught up in who you could've been
and disregarded my own privilege
just wanting to see you win
the pressure of wanting to save
all the while watching it all freeze over

—love them through it

In Bloom

i want to change everything
but i know i can't do it on my own
i have to be careful
not to be greedy with the space i occupy
sometimes it is more noble to keep quiet
i am not the authority on everything

—finding your voice means knowing when to use it, be a good ally

Reyna Noriega

how to

be happy?

choose it.

—it sounds too simple to be true

In Bloom

don't stunt your growth
thinking you know yourself

—keep learning

Reyna Noriega

you ask
why do i give away my secrets
why do i feed those
who may not give anything in return

—their success is my return, with or without a thank you

In Bloom

the first time i crossed paths
with a handsome stranger
that seemed to live a life
i would normally be curious about
curious enough to explore
and i was too caught up
in the fantasy of my own potential
too in love with the peace in my present
it was then i knew i was living right

—love will be real and not an escape

Reyna Noriega

there's a feeling i'm chasing
my home gives me that feeling
and the sea
my desk covered in art supplies
hugs from my family
it's a feeling i've yet to find in a man
and i won't settle until i have that

—love is all around me

In Bloom

i want the unicorn

—they are out there

Reyna Noriega

because i don't understand why i
of all people
could be chosen
to live this life
to know this truth
i walk
i create
i love
i share
like my days are numbered
like my blessings are numbered
i relinquish ego
and give myself up to service

—pay it forward

In Bloom

i make it look easy
perhaps
if you saw
oh if you saw
the situations i learned to stay calm in
remain grounded in trust
you'd be surprised

but why should i worry
when the universe
conspires with me
and all i really have to do,
is show up

—surrender was learned, and fortune replaced discomfort

Reyna Noriega

who am i?
nobody besides somebody
who lives life on her own terms
and that seems to be what they envy most
to fill my days and nights
exactly as i'd like
they'd say i crafted a life for myself
worth being envied
but i didn't craft anything
i merely surrendered

—surrender and beautiful things will happen

In Bloom

reframing what it means to facilitate change
or achieve a dream
reframing what i believe i need to do to,
have to do

following love and gratitude
applying surrender

it allows me to pivot,
it releases the restraints
allows me to flow effortlessly

—pivot

Reyna Noriega

gratitude
as i walk the loud city streets
everything i wanted
wishing to reach
now surrounds me
the knowing
recharges me

— i moved to the city

In Bloom

check your ego at the door
you don't need it here
move about the room with ease
everyone is just doing their best

—egos aren't welcome

Reyna Noriega

how could i know
the pain
the wounds
the scars
i thought were so ugly
i thought i should hide from
i thought somehow tainted me
would actually be the catalyst
of a beautiful evolution
a metamorphosis
a becoming

— i appreciate it all

In Bloom

it is so hard
to step out of the role
of being everyones savior
and say—
i want to be taught
i want to be heard
i want to be felt
and if you say
you can't,
or you're exhausted,
you become the villain

—doing what is necessary anyway

Reyna Noriega

love yourself more
than your idea of any person
go where there is love
ready to be given
ready to receive
ready to reciprocate

honor yourself
so you leave harmless patterns behind
no more convincing
no more
watering down your desires
for the sake of earning

i promise you
there is love
i promise you,
it's for you

—one thing i've learned

In Bloom

so strange to see them live
having let them go
but why should it be strange?
if not the catalyst for your own growth,
why should the experience only
grant you the wisdom
change requires?
how selfish,
how small to think
life would only be kind to you

and even if he gave her everything
he could never give you
you would remain
unbothered

—so what

Reyna Noriega

singing and dancing
i'm not sure what has come over me
why does it feel like suddenly
i have risen
chains
curses
no longer carrying the weights
of my ancestors
i am free

—broken curses

In Bloom

i will give
i will share
not for something in return
though you may not know how to receive
but because leading with kindness
will be my legacy
your prosperity,
will be my return

—learned selflessness

Reyna Noriega

no coincidences
1111
1234
1217
143

Thank you for speaking to me universe

—numbers are everywhere

In Bloom

Time
Is
Flying
Stop trying to catch it.

—make the most of it

Reyna Noriega

i don't really know how to teach happiness
i only know one day i was so tired
of being angry
jealous
lonely
tired of wanting to flee,
escape reality
waiting
for next
for more

i wanted peace
so i learned to accept where i was,
while gravitating towards more
i turned my light within
illuminating my strengths
and stopped bathing dark tunnels with that light
always searching
and not becoming

— i chose happiness aggressively

In Bloom

what a difference it can make
when you learn the function
of boundaries
when you no longer need to hide behind a list
of excuses and reasoning
you know exactly where you stand
rooted in your truth

—boundaries not barriers as heard on a podcast

Reyna Noriega

i deserve
i deserve this
because i've worked hard
i've cried hard
i've faced the harshest of truths
i stood up to my fears
i conquered the beast, the beast
that is self
so that i
fully formed
could stand before you today and say
i deserve

—love not luck

In Bloom

you may not want to make space for me,
but the universe has already carved out a path
for me

—move over

Reyna Noriega

so different
i was so different
things were so different
just a year ago
so many feelings have left
worry
envy
uncertainty
force

i have found my power
my flow
i have friendships lost to thank
and love disillusioned
and above all
my own bravery and commitment to self

—looking back

In Bloom

i am so proud of you,
you work so hard
you made a dream
we only whispered so long ago
a reality
and you aren't done yet

you are going to change the world
you are going to leave a legacy
but even better than that, i want you to know
i like it when you smile
i like it when you let your shoulders drop
i like it when you block out all the noise and listen
to your own voice

i love when you dance
i love when you go outside and feel the sun
i love when you laugh and your whole body
shakes

i love when you feel proud of us
i love it when you let go
we have grown so much
just look at our flower field

—a letter to me

Reyna Noriega

i found love
love through community
love in sisterhood
in conversations with mom
in puppy dog eyes
in the natural light in this house
home—
it is home
the sun the moon the stars
the green,
green everywhere
it surrounds me
it fills me
this is true love

—and it's better than i expected

In Bloom

pop a pill
drink the poison
self medicate to elevate
temporarily?

what good is that
when there are higher highs
longevity of suspension
in the air
and the drug is within
in the vaults
the parts of your mind
you dare not go

—how to elevate higher

Reyna Noriega

i'm so happy it never worked out
because now
when love finds me
i'll know—
that smile
i gave to myself first
as well as
all the treasures
i thought
only came with
Love

—i am a whole, waiting for a whole

In Bloom

I Love You
i say
to
the mirror

—and i mean it

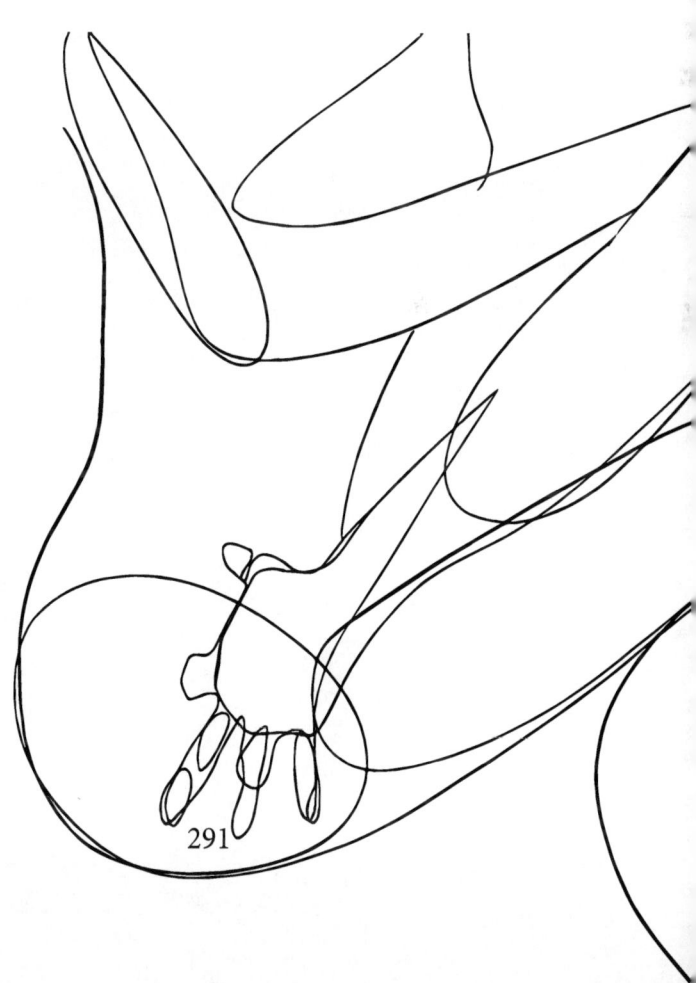

Reyna Noriega

how good it feels
to be outside
be alive
and just-
B R E A T H E

-gratitude

In Bloom

i
hate
 traff
ic so
i made
 my ow
n lane

—staying in my lane

Reyna Noriega

in circles surrounded by my sisters
i found healing and understanding
i would never have known
if i let them poison me
with lack
envy
competition
instead now
we are love
we are compassion
we are power

—sisterhood matters

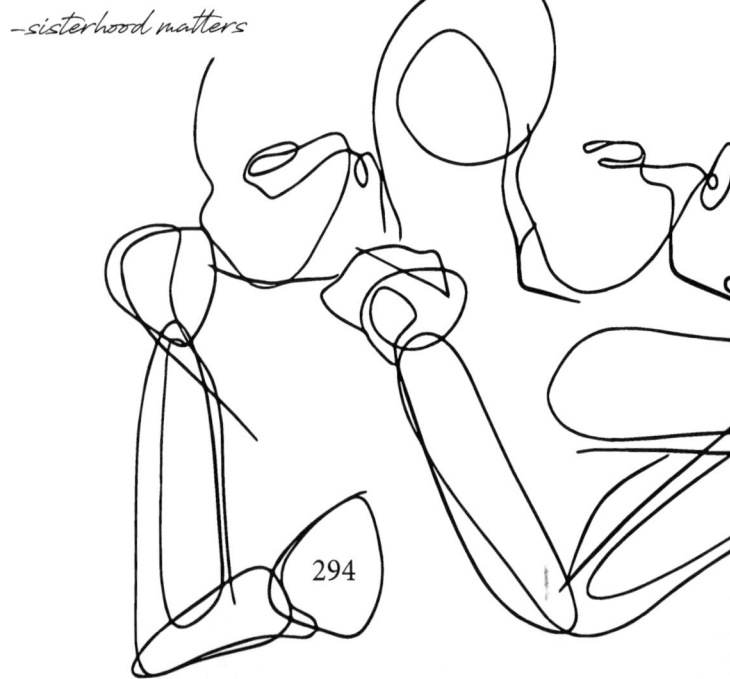

In Bloom

i once thought
the beauty of my heart
the rarity
needed to be protected
guarded
but it is expansive
infinite
perhaps my greatest power
and i will use it

—it is never ending

Reyna Noriega

thank you to the angel
that chose to possess me
open my eye
show me gratitude
i don't know
that i would've found my way
without you

—thank you

In Bloom

i love that i can breath here
reflect and stretch my wings here
i love that i can live loudly here
while also seeing peace reflected here
here is home
home is here

—finally a space the reflects my soul

Reyna Noriega

nothing beats
waking up
beautiful
not because my hair
is in tact
or my make up from the night before remains
but because in the first few moments
my first thoughts upon waking up
are filled with pride
rather than criticism
rather than curse my eyes for
their blurry view
express gratitude for they can see at all
instead of cursing my body
for how wide it is becoming
i acknowledge i feel
more of a woman
than i ever have

—morning loving

In Bloom

blueprints are everywhere
find them
use them
and know that you are never alone

—the path has been illuminated for you

Reyna Noriega

these are love letters to my universe
my partner in crime
i quite literally am nothing without you
thank you for whispering your secrets to me
showing me the way
using me as a vessel of light and truth
i will not dissapoint

—why me?

In Bloom

this time when they asked if i knew you
i didn't roll my eyes
i didn't exhale to show my disdain
knowing the conversation that always came next
a conversation i invited
this time instead i smiled
not for you
but internally
because the growth
i've known since you
has been so precious to me
i no longer feel the need
to smear your name
or entertain them
with stories of our past

—i don't want to talk about you anymore

Reyna Noriega

it was a good day
when i could put away inspiration
take down my moodboard
all the concepts
i should try
learn
and instead, just
be

—i am my own mood

In Bloom

going through hard times without mama
i'm reminded
i can
i'm capable
i'm strong
she raised me that way

and even at times
i can't find it in me
to understand
to excuse
i can still appreciate
that much

—epiphany moment

Reyna Noriega

look at me
giving myself everything
i thought i could only get
from a man

—*who would've thought?*

In Bloom

And all at once
I feel free
And the tears that fall
Are a result of the release
They dance down and merge
With the anointing from the shower head

No longer defined by past love
No longer afraid to mess up
To not be enough
I am whole
I am whole
I am whole

And because i never want to be half again
I will love a full whole being
I am deserving
And capable
And ready

No longer questioning
Am i fun enough ?
Sexy enough?
Giving enough

I am me
Enough.

Reyna Noriega

honor your journey
because you wouldn't be
here now
if you hadn't been
there then

—each step is precious

In Bloom

before checking off
the list of superficials
or the condensed list
of the characteristics
Breath
Pause
Fall in like
Fall in trust
Leave room to choose

—this time will be different

Reyna Noriega

never again will i sell myself the lie
that i can be too busy for love
that comes with weighing down my heart
like holding a float under
why, if that is not its purpose?

the truth remains
no matter how busy
i still think of you
i still dream of you
i still long for you

—still you

In Bloom

I'm grateful to look around and love
And trust
To see the world in colors
In auras
To live
To exist
To experience
To take in breaths slower
To slowly lose tension
Resentment
Anger
Doubt
I feel myself become lighter
And with it limitless
I am carried by the wind
I am held up by love
I am supported by the universe

— I take comfort in this

Reyna Noriega

You're beautiful
All of you
The weight you haven't loss yet
The scar that is still fading
I love your lashes that are maybe too short
Your eyebrows too thin
And the laugh lines beginning to come in
They are enough
They are more than enough by the only standards that matter

—*your own*

In Bloom

Wear your crown proudly
You fought for it
You've earned it
It is rightfully yours

—it's golden, you're golden

Reyna Noriega

How lucky are YOU
that YOU get to be with
ME

—perspective shift

In Bloom

who would've thought
talking to you
just talking to you
like a normal human being
cures all these feelings
the desperation
the longing
the helplessness
it helps me to see things more clear

—my imagination was in control, but no more

Reyna Noriega

all of
the layers
we must
rip off
to reveal
what has
been there
all along

we are
divine.

—always have been, always will be

In Bloom

when i journal
i dont make a list
i don't make demands
i just
say

thank you.

thank you

Reyna Noriega

Releasing all fears and anchors.

I'm ready to be weightless and fearless.

Because I know you are actively preparing my harvest I ask that in the meantime you prepare my mind body and spirit.

This is the part of my journey where things get more interesting. Where the curses I've broken make way for real blessings.

I have a pull to travel, I don't know why, but it's there. It's always been there and if it is apart of fulfilling my purpose and destiny, I feel I am about to find out.

Keep me safe.
Keep me light
Move through me.

I am ready. I am Love.

In Bloom

Put me in a new pot.

In the months to come I hope I meet Reyna, REYNA. Reyna in her fullest form to date.

She is confident.
She is focused.
She is strong.
She is unapologetically herself.

I am so grateful to meet her.
So grateful to BE her.

Grateful.

-Moving.
Journal 11.12.2019

Reyna Noriega

don't be so fucused on the results of my inner work you miss how i got here to begin with.

focus on you
water you
i'm rooting for YOU.

—good luck

In Bloom

Hey Reyna, how are you :)
1 unread whatsapp message

Reyna Noriega

in case you missed it ...

surrender

abundance

LOVE

boundaries

In Bloom

remember these words.

gratitude

PEACE

Photographed by: Kovalski Jacques

about the AUTHOR

Reyna Noriega is an author, illustrator, and educator. For her, art has always been a tool by which she could dive deeper into herself. The joy and clarity it brings her has led her to devote her work to help others heal and find happiness that is intrinsic. She lets her culture and experiences as a black latinx woman shine through in her work in the hopes others can see representation for their experiences and feel empowered.

In her writing she contemplates the human emotional and spiritual existance, taking her readers through her various life lessons in the hope of leaving a blueprint for others on their personal journey.

Today she continues to create, take clients, and publish books that quench her thirst for creativity.

www.reynanoriega.com
come say hi!

Made in the USA
San Bernardino, CA
02 June 2020